This book belongs to

D1085538

_____

_____

Seven Sabeels Press

السلام عليكم

Assalamualaikum,

May peace be upon you.

If you and your child enjoyed this

book and found it beneficial,

please help us to leave a review.

Thank you!

جزاك الله خير

Written by: Sheila Ibrahim
Illustrated by: Tony Surya

Paperback ISBN: 9798427253680
E-book ISBN: B09TZHVZCV

Let's Learn More about Ramadan

"When Ramadan begins, the gates of Paradise are opened."

~ Prophet Muhammad (PBUH) ~

Narrated by Abu Huraira. Sahih al-Bukhari 1898.

It was a Saturday afternoon and Sumayya was spending the weekend at her grandparent's home.

"Grandma! Grandpa! Isn't it time for our tea break?" asked Sumayya.

"Can we go down to the café for pancakes, please?"

"Oh Sumayya, we can't. Grandpa and I are fasting today," replied Grandma.

"Fasting? What does that mean?" asked Sumayya.

"That means we do not eat or drink from dawn until sunset."

"No food or drink?" Sumayya wondered aloud.

"That's right," said Grandpa. "But usually, we wake up early to have our *suhoor*, which is the morning meal before dawn."

"Just for today?"

"No, dear. We, Muslims, fast for one whole month," explained Grandma. "The month of fasting is called *Ramadan*."

Sumayya's eyes widened with curiosity. "Can you tell me more about Ramadan?"

"Of course, sweetheart," said Grandpa. "Let Grandma and I finish reading the Qur'an, and then we'll tell you more."

Sumayya went back to work on her jigsaw puzzle. Moments later, she heard a crash. Kitty, the cat, had jumped across the coffee table and knocked over Grandma's favorite vase.

"Kitty! You, naughty cat!" shouted Sumayya.

"Don't shout, Sumayya dear," said Grandma, as she picked up the broken pieces.

"Why aren't you angry, Grandma?" asked Sumayya. "Isn't that your favorite vase?"

"Yes, it is," replied Grandma. "Come here, let's us tell you more about Ramadan."

Sumayya became excited and went to sit beside Grandma.
"Although we fast to know what it's like to be hungry and to be thankful for the food we have, Ramadan is much more than that."
"What else is Ramadan about?" asked Sumayya eagerly.

"Ramadan is also about practicing self-control and self-discipline to avoid doing things that Allah does not like," explained Grandma. "For example, I stopped myself from losing my temper even though Kitty broke my favorite vase."

"You can say 'I am fasting' aloud as a reminder to be patient," Grandpa chimed in. "But I'm not fasting, Grandpa!" said Sumayya. "Will Allah be mad at me?"

"Of course not, sweetheart. Not everyone needs to fast," replied Grandpa. "For example, little kids, pregnant women, and those who are ill, need not fast."

Later that afternoon, Sumayya completed the puzzle,
after which she became restless and bored.
"Grandpa, let's go down to the lake to watch the ducks!"
suggested Sumayya.

"Maybe next time. I'm going around the neighborhood to give out some dates and water," said Grandpa. "Would you like to join me?" Sumayya frowned. That did not sound like fun.

"Don't be upset, Sumayya," said Grandma. "Ramadan is a month of giving."

"Allah likes those who are generous to people in need. By helping others, we are also expressing our gratitude to Him," said Grandpa. "Aren't you grateful for all that you have?"

Sumayya thought about all that she had and felt embarrassed.

"*Alhamdullilah*, I have all that I need and more," said Sumayya. "Let's go and help others, Grandpa!"

Along the way, Sumayya noticed that people would smile and say "Ramadan Mubarak" to each other.

"Why do they say 'Ramadan Mubarak'?" she asked.

Grandpa smiled. "It's a way to wish someone a blessed Ramadan!"

When they reached home, Grandma was putting food on the dining table.

"Grandma, is it dinner already?" asked Sumayya.

"*Iftar*," corrected Grandma with a smile. "It's the evening meal to break our fast."

Grandpa turned on the radio, and the *adhan* started to play. He and Grandma raised their hands to say a *dua* before breaking their fast with a piece of date each.

Later that evening, Sumayya followed her grandparents to the mosque. While there, she saw them reciting *dhikr* and putting money in the donation box.

They also stayed back after the *Isha* prayer to perform many more *raka'ahs* together.

On the way back from the mosque, Sumayya could not control her curiosity. "Grandpa, why were there extra prayers?"

"Ramadan is a month of blessings when rewards are multiplied," explained Grandpa. "That's why we try hard to increase our acts of worship and good deeds. Like performing extra prayers called *Taraweeh*."

"And *InshaAllah*, He will forgive all of our sins," added Grandma. "Do you know that Ramadan is a month of forgiveness, too?"

Sumayya nodded her head. She finally knew why her grandparents spent time reading the Qur'an, reciting *dhikr*, distributing food, and donating money.

"What a special month!" exclaimed Sumayya.

"Indeed, it is," said Grandma. "After all, Ramadan is the month when the Qur'an was sent down."

"I think I understand now," said Sumayya as they entered the house. "Allah has blessed us to see another month of Ramadan because He loves us and wants us to become a better person."

"That's right, sweetheart," said Grandpa. "Allah is the most merciful."

At bedtime, Sumayya kissed her grandparents goodnight. "Grandma, Grandpa, do you think you can wake me up for *suhoor*? I would like to try to fast so that I can please Allah."

Her grandparents smiled and tucked her into bed.

"Of course, *InshaAllah*," said Grandma.

"Goodnight and Ramadan Mubarak to you, my dear," whispered Grandpa.

Glossary

- Fasting: Fasting in Islam means no eating or drinking from dawn till sunset.

- Suhoor: Suhoor is the morning meal served before dawn during Ramadan. Waking up early to have Suhoor is important to ensure enough energy for the day ahead.

- Ramadan: Ramadan is a holy month of fasting for Muslims. It is also the ninth month in the Muslim calendar.

- Alhamdullilah: Alhamdullilah is an Arabic phrase that means "praise be to Allah." It is usually said to express relief and thanks to Allah (SWT).

- Ramadan Mubarak: "Mubarak" means "blessed" in Arabic. Thus, "Ramadan Mubarak" is a greeting used during the fasting month to wish someone a blessed Ramadan.

Glossary

- **Iftar:** Iftar is the evening meal served at sunset during Ramadan to break the day's fast. Muslims usually break their fast at home or at their local mosque.

- **Adhan:** The adhan is the Islamic call to invite Muslims to perform their obligatory prayers. During Ramadan, the sound of adhan during the evening indicates the time for Muslims to break their fast.

- **Dua:** Dua is a form of worship done by raising the hands to call out to Allah. Making dua is how Muslims connect with Allah (SWT), remember Him, and have conversations with Him. Muslims usually make dua to ask Allah (SWT) for help and to seek His forgiveness.

- **Dhikr:** Dhikr is a form of worship that refers to the act of remembering Allah (SWT) by reciting short prayers repeatedly aloud or silently. This act is usually accompanied with prayer beads to count the number of prayers recited.

Glossary

- Isha prayer: The Isha prayer is one of the five daily obligatory prayers. It is also the last prayer of the day, and it is performed at night.

- Raka'ah: Raka'ah refers to a singular cycle of movement in an Islamic prayer.

- Taraweeh: Taraweeh is the special prayers during Ramadan conducted after the Isha prayer that Muslims are strongly encouraged to perform to seek extra rewards.

- InshaAllah: InshaAllah is an Arabic phrase that means "If God wills it" and it is used when talking about a situation in the future.

Summary

What is Ramadan all about?

1) To develop a sense of empathy and gratitude

Fasting during Ramadan allows us to understand what it is like to go hungry. Consequently, we develop a deep sense of empathy towards the less fortunate and a sense of gratitude for the food we get.

2) To strive to become a better person

Ramadan is also about practicing self-control and self-discipline. We can break bad habits and replace them with good ones by consistently being conscious of our actions, thoughts, and behavior.

3) To self-reflect and strengthen our connection with Allah (SWT)

Ramadan is a month for us to slow down and seek nearness to Allah (SWT) by reflecting on our relationship with Him and increasing our acts of worship.

Summary

What should Muslims strive to do during Ramadan?

1) Increase acts of worship

- Recite the Qur'an & perform dhikr

- Perform extra Taraweeh prayers

2) Increase good deeds

- Be charitable and generous

- Donate food and money to people less fortunate

3) Improve oneself and avoid bad behavior

- Be kind, patient, and polite

- Avoid gossiping, idle talks, and foul words

- Control your temper and say "I am fasting" aloud when provoked to be reminded of the best conduct a person should practice while fasting

[According to a sunnah narrated by Abu Huraira. Source: Sahih al-Bukhari 1984]

Summary

Why is Ramadan such a special month for Muslims?

1) It is a month of giving and charity
- Ramadan is the month to be more generous than ever, give back to society, and care for the less fortunate.

2) It is a month of mercy and forgiveness
- Ramadan is the month to not only seek mercy and forgiveness from Allah for past sins, but also to forgive others and reconcile relationships.

3) It is a month of blessings and rewards
- Ramadan is the month of great blessings when rewards for good deeds, acts of worship, and simple acts of kindness are multiplied immensely.

4) It is a month of reflection and the Holy Qur'an
- Ramadan is the month where the Holy Qur'an was first sent down and revealed to Prophet Muhammad (PBUH). Thus, Ramadan is a great opportunity to reconnect with the Qur'an and develop a stronger connection with Allah (SWT) by reflecting on the meaning of His words.

OTHER BOOKS BY SEVEN SABEELS PRESS

  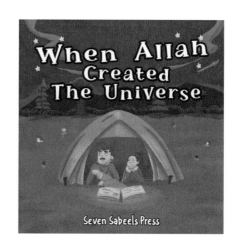

**Let's Learn More About
Eid al-Adha**

**When Allah Created
The Universe**

**How To Deal With Anger
The Islamic Way**

If you and your child enjoyed
this book and found it beneficial,
please help us to leave a review.
Thank you!

جزاك الله خير

69632443R00026